Reading and Writing Poetry

Poem selections and activities by Maria Backus

Illustrations by Ann Stein

Project Manager: Mina McMullin

Editor: Kathy Zaun

Production and Design: Jill Kaufman, Jennifer Sottoriva

Cover Design: Signature Design Group, Inc.

GOOD APPLE
A Division of Frank Schaffer Publications, Inc.
23740 Hawthorne Blvd.
Torrance, CA 90505

ISBN 1-56417-959-1

Table of Contents

Y ou will be amazed at how much fun poetry can be for students! *Reading and Writing Poetry* gives students hands-on practice in reading and writing poetry of all kinds. It is the perfect way for them to learn about both poetry and literary forms.

This book is divided into 12 chapters. The first six each feature a poem (or part of one) to teach students about the important literary forms of personification, metaphor, irony, alliteration, onomatopoeia, and hyperbole. Also in each of these chapters is information about the literary form and the featured poem, objectives, student activities, a student activity page, and a "sampler" containing examples of the literary form. All of these components enable students to better understand and to more comfortably write their own examples of these literary forms.

The next six chapters each focus on one of these types of poems: haiku, narrative, free verse, limerick, lyric, cinquain. A poem is presented at the front of each chapter, and each chapter also contains facts about the poem form, objectives, information about the poem itself, notes for reading and writing poems, a "sampler" consisting of examples of the featured poetry form, and a student activity page. All of these components allow students to enjoy themselves as they gain a greater understanding of poetry and learn to write poems of their own.

As students begin to relax and enjoy writing poetry and using the featured literary forms, help them create their own poetry books or journals. To do this, give students copies of page 56. Then have them write a sample of each literary form and type of poetry on these pages. Next, assemble the pages into book form.

This book truly provides students with an exciting and stimulating means for them to learn to enjoy poetry and literature.

The Musical Lion

by Oliver Herford

Said the Lion, "On music I dote
But something is wrong with my throat.
When I practice a scale,
The listeners quail,
And flee at the very first note!"

FACTS ABOUT PERSONIFICATION

Personification is a literary device that gives human qualities such as emotions, intelligence, personality, or form to animals, ideas, or inanimate objects. Personification extends our human experience to non-humans. This helps us better understand and appreciate our human qualities.

Read the poem "The Musical Lion" with the students and ask for their reactions. Do they think the poem is humorous? How does the personification of the lion affect students? Do they feel sorry for the lion?

OBJECTIVES

- To introduce personification in a literary context
- To present examples of personification in well-known poems
- To encourage students to use personification in writing
- To show how personification adds interest and variety to language

PERSONIFICATION SAMPLER

Give each student a copy of the Personification Sampler on page 7. The first poem by Carl Sandburg, "Under a Telephone Wire," personifies an inanimate object. The second poem by Sandburg, "Proud Words," personifies the abstract idea "proud words." After students react to the poems, have them discuss the use of personification in both poems. "The Puzzled Centipede" and "Alas, Alack!" are short, humorous poems students will also enjoy.

Give students a copy of page 56 to use to write their own examples of personification after completing page 8.

SUGGESTED ACTIVITIES

1. Let students discuss how and why people use personification. Ask them to give examples from literature (stories such as *Charlotte's Web*, or *The Wind in the Willows*) or their own lives.

2. Show students a picture of a daffodil, then read the Mother Goose version of "Daffadowndilly" below.

Daffadowndilly
  Has come to town,
In a yellow petticoat
  And a green gown.

Growing in the vale
  By the uplands hilly,
Growing straight and frail,
Lady Daffadowndilly.

In a golden crown,
And a scant green gown
  While the spring blows chilly,
Lady Daffadown,
  Sweet Daffadowndilly.

Discuss the personification and the rich use of detail in this poem. Ask students what they like about this poem.

3. As a class activity, have students suggest ways to personify a rock, a tree, a flower, the wind, and a fox. For example, a tree might be personified as being strong, proud, dignified, wise, happy to be a home for birds, irritated by crawling insects, frightened of being cut down, etc. Have students select one of these topics and write a short poem or story that includes some personification.

ACTIVITY PAGE 8

Students first personify an inanimate object and write a story from its point of view. Then they personify an animal and write a story from its point of view.

Personification Sampler

Under a Telephone Wire

I am a copper wire slung in the air,
Slim against the sun I make not even a clear line of shadow.
Night and day I keep singing—humming and thrumming;
It is love and war and money; it is fighting and the tears, the work and the want,
Death and laughter of men and women passing through me, carrier of your speech,
In the rain and the wet dripping, in the dawn and shine drying,
A copper wire.

—*Carl Sandburg*

Proud Words

Look out how you use proud words.
When you let proud words go, it is not easy to call them back.
They wear long boots, hard boots, they walk off proud; they can't hear you calling—
Look out how you use proud words.

—*Carl Sandburg*

The Puzzled Centipede

A centipede was happy quite,
Until a frog in fun
Said, "Pray, which leg comes after which?"
This raised her mind to such a pitch,
She lay distracted in the ditch
Considering how to run.

Alas, Alack!

Ann, Ann!
   Come quick as you can!
There's a fish that *talks*
   In the frying pan.
Out of the fat,
   As clear as glass,
He put up his mouth
   And moaned "Alas!"
Oh, most mournful,
   "Alas, alack!"
Then turned to his sizzling
   And sank him back.

—*Walter de la Mare*

NAME _____

So Humanlike!

Everyone has a story to tell—and perhaps every thing does, too. For example, if a skyscraper could talk, it might tell a story something like this:

From way up here, I can see out over the whole city. In the morning, the bright sunshine reflected in my windows makes me glow for miles. At night, I have a million little lights inside me to brighten up the skyline. I am the tallest of all the towers, and probably the most handsome! I try to stand straight and tall and proud—to do my best to help my little city below.

The skyscraper in this story was personified with many human qualities. List two of these human qualities on the lines below.

_____

_____

Choose one of the items below and write the story that it might tell. Personify the item by giving it **several** human qualities. Use the back of this paper to plan and write your story.

an ancient sequoia tree
Thomas Jefferson's fountain pen
Betsy Ross's thimble
Babe Ruth's bat
John Glenn's space capsule
Madame Curie's laboratory
a cowboy's lasso
Thurgood Marshall's gavel

Amazing Animals

If animals could talk, they would probably have interesting stories to tell about people. Choose one of the animals from the list below. Then write a story the animal might tell about the people in its life.

a spider building a web
a pigeon in a city
a duck in the park
a mouse in a church
an ant at a picnic

Write the first draft of the story on a piece of scrap paper. Revise and edit your story. Then write the final version on another piece of paper. Share your story with your classmates.

Dreams
by Langston Hughes

Hold fast to dreams
    For if dreams die
        Life is a broken-winged bird
        That cannot fly.

Hold fast to dreams
    For when dreams go
        Life is a barren field
        Frozen with snow.

FACTS ABOUT METAPHORS

A metaphor is a literary device that compares two unlike items. For example, in the metaphor, *the bullfrog's croak was the tuba of the swamp band*, the low croaking sound of a bullfrog is compared to the low sound of a tuba. Unlike similes, metaphors do not use the words "like" or "as" to compare the two items.

Although many metaphors have been overused and have become cliches, original metaphors can make language vivid and give us new insights.

The poem on page 9, "Dreams," was written by Langston Hughes. Read the poem to the students and have them identify and discuss the two metaphors: *life is a broken-winged bird that cannot fly* and *life is a barren field frozen with snow.* Ask students if they agree with Hughes' ideas about a life without dreams. To what else could life without dreams be compared?

OBJECTIVES

- To introduce metaphors in a literary context
- To present examples of metaphors in well-known poems
- To encourage students to use metaphors in writing
- To show students how metaphors can add interest and variety to language

METAPHOR SAMPLER

Before giving copies of the Metaphor Sampler on page 12 to your students, read the poem "Steam Shovel" by Charles Malam. However, do not tell them the title. Ask them to listen closely and identify the metaphor in the poem.

The poem "Mother to Son," was also written by Langston Hughes. Have students react to the poem and identify this metaphor: *Life ain't been no crystal stair.* You may need to talk about the use of dialect in this poem.

The short poem "Fog" is one of Carl Sandburg's most well-known poems. Encourage students to write a similar metaphor poem describing wind, thunder, sleet, or snow.

Give students a copy of page 56 to use to write a finished poem containing a metaphor. Tell them that they can write the poem they compose after completing activity page 13, or they can write a different one.

Metaphor

SUGGESTED ACTIVITIES

1. Many metaphors have been so overused that they have become worn out. Have your students brainstorm a list of as many overused metaphors as they know, then discuss the ones below.

   He's the backbone of society.

   He's a snake in the grass.

   This place is a zoo!

   She's a big fish in a small pond.

   She's a clown.

   He's the life of the party.

2. Help students learn to distinguish between metaphors and similes by discussing the sentences below. Then ask students to explain the meaning of each metaphor or simile.

   Your education is your ticket to the future. (metaphor)

   The clouds were like puffs of cotton, floating in the summer sky. (simile)

   The old crate was the little boy's castle. (metaphor)

   Like a pendulum of a grandfather clock, the conductor's arms swung in time to the music. (simile)

   The road stretched ahead like silver ribbon in the moonlight. (simile)

   The old diary was a window to the past. (metaphor)

3. Let students work in pairs to complete each statement below with a metaphor. Then assemble the entire class and let students share their results.

   Grandma's hair was a . . .

   The garden was a . . .

   The hole under the tree was the . . .

   The old chair was Grandpa's . . .

   The ancient tree was a . . .

ACTIVITY PAGE 13

Tell students to first read Vachel Lindsay's poem, "The Moon's the North Wind's Cooky." Next, they answer several questions about this poem and then proceed to write their own moon metaphor poems. Note: Since Vachel Lindsay's poem also contains some personification, you may want to review this figure of speech with your students before they complete the activity. (See pages 5–8.)

Metaphor Sampler

Steam Shovel

The dinosaurs are not all dead.
I saw one raise its iron head
To watch me walking down the road
Beyond our house today.
Its jaws were dripping with a load
Of earth and grass that it had cropped.
It must have heard me where I stopped,
Snorted white steam my way,
And stretched its long neck out to see,
And chewed, and grinned quite amiably.

—*Charles Malam*

Fog

The fog comes
on little cat feet.

It sits looking
over harbor and city
on silent haunches
and then, moves on.

—*Carl Sandburg*

Mother to Son

Well, son, I'll tell you:
Life for me ain't been no crystal stair.
It's had tacks in it,
And splinters,
And boards torn up,
And places with no carpet on the floor—
Bare.
But all the time
I'se been a-climbin' on,
And reachin' landin's
And turnin' corners,
And sometimes goin' in the dark
Where there ain't been no light.
So boy, don't you turn back.
Don't you set down on the steps
'Cause you finds it's kinder hard.
Don't you fall now—
For I'se still goin', honey,
I'se still climbin',
And life for me ain't been no crystal stair.

—*Langston Hughes*

NAME _____

Can You Compare?

Read the poem below, "The Moon's the North Wind's Cooky."
Then answer the questions that follow it.

The Moon's the North Wind's Cooky (What the Little Girl Said)

The Moon's the North Wind's Cooky.
He bites it, day by day,
Until there's but a rim of scraps
That crumble all away.

The South Wind is a baker.
He kneads clouds in his den,
And bakes a crisp new moon that . . . greedy
North . . . Wind . . . eats . . . again!

—*Vachel Lindsay*

1. From whose point of view is Vachel Lindsay writing?

   _____

2. To what does Vachel Lindsay compare the moon?

   _____

3. Do you think this metaphor is original and effective? Why or why not?

   _____

   _____

4. Lindsay has also used personification in this poem. List one example of personification in the poem.

   _____

5. In other poems, Vachel Lindsay has compared the moon to a cottage with a door and to a griffin's egg. (A griffin is an imaginary animal with its head, forepart, and wings like those of an eagle, and its body, hind legs, and tail like those of a lion.) To what else do you think the moon could be compared? List several ideas.

   _____

6. Select one of your ideas and write it as a metaphor.

   _____

7. On the back of this page, write the first draft of a short poem containing a metaphor about the moon. Then team up with a writing partner to revise and edit your poem. Write the final version on another piece of paper and share it with your class. You may want to include an illustration with your poem.

The Crocodile
by Lewis Carroll

How doth the little crocodile
    Improve his shining tail,
        And pour the waters of the Nile
        On every golden scale!

How cheerfully he seems to grin,
    How neatly spreads his claws,
        And welcomes little fishes in,
        With gently smiling jaws!

FACTS ABOUT IRONY

Verbal irony is a literary form that lets us say one thing but mean the opposite. Usually irony is expressed in positive words, but it implies blame. Irony is lighter in tone than sarcasm, but it can be more cutting! There can also be irony in an event or situation in which the result is the opposite of what we expect to happen.

You may want to ask students if they have heard the term *crocodile tears*. Ask them how the term relates to the Lewis Carroll poem "The Crocodile." Then ask them to describe the ironic situations in this poem.

OBJECTIVES

- To introduce irony in a literary context
- To present examples of irony in well-known stories and poems
- To encourage students to use irony in writing
- To show students how irony can add interest and variety to language

IRONY SAMPLER

Give each student a copy of the Irony Sampler on page 16. The first poem, "The Crocodile," is by Lewis Carroll. The second poem, "The Frogs Who Wanted a King," is based on one of Aesop's fables. Let students discuss the irony in both poems.

Give students a copy of page 56. On the page, have students include their own examples of irony which they can write after they have completed activity page 17.

SUGGESTED ACTIVITIES

1. Tell students that Aesop was a slave who lived in Greece over 2600 years ago. The many stories he told in the streets and marketplaces of Athens were based on what he had observed and knew about people.

One of Aesop's stories was about a man that had a hen that laid golden eggs. The man thought the hen must be solid gold on the inside. He killed the hen only to find that it was no different than any other hen. The man hoped to gain an instant fortune, but instead he lost a fine daily income.

Ask students to discuss the irony in this story. You might also want students to discuss the *moral* of the story and how it could be applied to their lives.

2. Let students discuss in what situations they might say the following phrases but actually *mean* the opposite:

   Nice job.
   Way to go.
   Super.
   That's just great.
   Wow.

   Ask students what other expressions they sometimes use that mean the opposite of what they say. What part does intonation play in verbal irony?

3. Have students work in pairs to write a short ironic story. If they need a story idea, suggest one of the following:

   a "friendly" octopus
   someone who gets his or her wish, but not quite in the expected way
   the "perfect" picnic

ACTIVITY PAGE 17

Students note the ironic elements in three of *Aesop's Fables*.

Irony Sampler

The Crocodile

How doth the little crocodile
    Improve his shining tail,
And pour the waters of the Nile
    On every golden scale!

How cheerfully he seems to grin,
    How neatly spreads his claws,
And welcomes little fishes in,
    With gently smiling jaws!

—*Lewis Carroll*

The Frogs Who Wanted a King

The frogs were living happy as could be
    In a wet marsh to which they all were suited;
From every sort of trouble they were free,
    and all night long they croaked, and honked, and hooted;
But one fine day a bull frog said, "The thing
We never had and *must* have is a king."

So all the frogs immediately prayed;
    "Great Jove," they chorused from their swampy border,
"Send us a king and he will be obeyed,
    A king to bring a rule of Law and Order."
Jove heard and chuckled. That night in the bog
There fell a large and most impressive Log.

The swamp was silent; nothing breathed. At first
    The baldly frightened frogs did never *once* stir;
But gradually some neared and even durst
    To touch, aye, even dance upon, the monster.
Whereat they croaked again, "Great Jove, oh hear!
Send us a *living* king, a king to fear!"

Once more Jove smiled, and sent them down a Stork,
    "Long live–!" they croaked. But ere they framed the sentence,
The stork bent down and, scorning knife or fork,
    Swallowed them all, with no time for repentance!

The moral's this: No matter what your lot,
It might be worse. Be glad with what you've got.

—*Joseph Lauren*

How Ironic!

Each story below is from *Aesop's Fables*. Examine the situation in each story, then describe the irony.

✦⟣⟠⟣✦

Who could run faster? Back and forth the tortoise and the hare argued! To end the argument, they decided to have a race. The hare was so confident of victory that he lay down by the side of the road and took a nap. As the tortoise approached the finish line on the gravel road, the hare was just waking up from a nap in the soft bed of bright spring flowers. The hare looked in surprise at the tortoise. The tortoise crawled without pausing and crossed the finish line first.

_____

_____

_____

_____

✦⟣⟠⟣✦

"What luck!" the crow thought. "I have found a snake to eat for supper." As the crow flew off with the snake, the snake coiled around, reached back, and bit the crow.

_____

_____

_____

_____

✦⟣⟠⟣✦

A deer was proud of its beautiful strong antlers but ashamed of its scrawny legs. When a lion chased him, however, the deer ran and quickly outdistanced the lion on the open ground. But the lion kept chasing the deer until they entered a forest. The deer's large antlers quickly got caught in the branches of a tree.

_____

_____

_____

_____

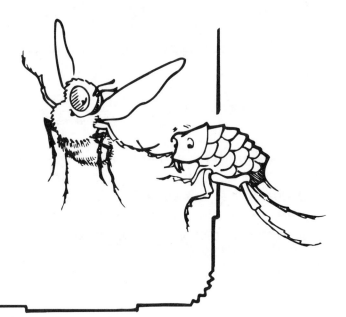

The Flea and the Fly

A flea and a fly got caught in a flue.
Said the fly, "Let us flee."
Said the flea, "Let us fly."
So together they flew through a flaw in the flue.

FACTS ABOUT ALLITERATION

Alliteration is a literary term in which an initial identical consonant sound is repeated. An example is this: *The willows were whispering in the wind.* When alliteration is used well, it not only adds interest and variety to language, it also lets us appreciate the sounds and beauty of words.

The lines above are from a humorous poem, "The Flea and the Fly." Read and talk about the poem with the students. Then discuss the examples of alliteration in the poem.

Alliteration

OBJECTIVES

- To introduce alliteration in a literary context
- To present examples of alliteration in well-known poems
- To encourage students to use alliteration in writing
- To show students how alliteration can add interest and variety to language

ALLITERATION SAMPLER

Give each student a copy of the Alliteration Sampler on page 20. First, read each poem with the students and ask for reactions. What do students like or dislike about the poems? How do the poems make them feel? What words do they like in the poems? Then ask students to identify the examples of alliteration in each poem. Some students may enjoy illustrating "The Eagle" or "White Butterflies." Students can add their own examples of alliteration to a copy of page 56 after they complete activity page 21.

SUGGESTED ACTIVITIES

1. Obtain several poetry books from your library. Let pairs of students browse through the books looking for examples of alliteration. Make a classroom chart to record the examples students find. Encourage students to read favorite poems to the class.

2. Ask students to add alliterative words to the sentences below.

> **Example:**
> **One by one, the leaves fell from the maple tree.**
> **One by one, the *large* leaves fell from the *mighty* maple tree.**

My little brother always has something to say.
The drive to Grandma's house took a long time.
The hamburger was greasy.
We helped our neighbors move into (or out of) their house.

Share the sample sentences with the class.

3. Write the following sentence on the board and have students copy it onto a sheet of paper: *"Twas in the month of May."* Have students skip three or four lines, then copy this sentence: *"All in all, it was a* (pick one: *dark* or *delightful*) *day."* Tell students that they now have the beginning and the ending of a poem or story. Let pairs of students work together to write the middle section. Encourage students to use some alliteration in their poems or stories. Have students read their work to their classmates.

ACTIVITY PAGE 21

Students first experiment with alliteration by completing phrases and sentences. Then students write an alliteration name poem.

Alliteration Sampler

Precious Stones

An emerald is as green as grass;
A ruby red as blood;
A sapphire shines as blue as heaven;
A flint lies in the mud.

A diamond is a brilliant stone;
To catch the world's desire;
An opal holds a fiery spark;
But a flint holds fire.

—*Christina Georgina Rossetti*

The Eagle

He clasps the crag with crooked hands;
Close to the sun in lonely lands,
Ringed with the azure world, he stands.

The wrinkled sea beneath him crawls;
He watches from his mountain walls,
And like a thunderbolt he falls.

—*Alfred, Lord Tennyson*

White Butterflies

Fly, white butterflies, out to sea,
Frail, pale wings for the wind to try,
Small, white wings that we scarce can see,
    Fly!

Some fly light as a laugh of glee,
Some fly soft as a long, low sigh;
All to the haven where each would be,
    Fly!

—*Algernon Charles Swinburne*

NAME _____

Fun With Letters

Alliteration can add variety and interest to language. It can also be fun to write. In the examples below, fill in each blank with a word of your choice that starts with the indicated letter.

1. a plaid, purple p_____

2. soft, silent s_____

3. baseball and b_____

4. w_____, white, w_____

5. a river r_____

6. curly c_____

7. jumping j_____

8. a m_____ mess

9. the last l_____

10. a terrible t_____

"Roy raced recklessly on his rollerblades."

On the lines below, complete the sentences by writing words that begin with the indicated letters.

11. Messy M_____ made more messes in the month of M_____ than

    M_____ , M_____ , and M_____ all made in the month of

    M_____ .

12. My dog D_____ danced with D_____ , the d_____ .

13. For supper, P_____ ate p_____ p_____ and p_____ .

On the back of this page, write an alliterative "name poem." First, write each letter of your first name on a separate line. Next to each letter, write a description of yourself using at least two words that start with that letter. The name "Sam" is done as an example below.

S—SOMETIMES SERIOUS, SOMETIMES SILLY

A—ALWAYS ALERT AND ACTIVE

M—MAGNIFICENT, BUT MESSY

from *"The Bells"*

by Edgar Allan Poe

Hear the sledges with their bells—
  Silver bells!
What a world of merriment their melody foretells!
  How they tinkle, tinkle, tinkle,
    In the icy air of night!
  While the stars that oversprinkle
  All the heavens, seem to twinkle
    With a crystalline delight;
  Keeping time, time, time,
  In a sort of Runic rhyme,
To the tintinnabulation that so musically wells
  From the bells, bells, bells, bells
    Bells, bells, bells—
From the jingling and the tinkling of the bells.

FACTS ABOUT ONOMATOPOEIA

Onomatopoeia is a literary form in which words sound like their meaning. Some examples are "snap," "hiss," "bang," "clash," "boom," "thud," "buzz," and "sizzle." These types of words are used not only in poetry, but in everyday speech. Onomatopoeia makes our language fun to say and hear.

The poem above is an excerpt from Edgar Allan Poe's poem, "The Bells." Ask students to identify any onomatopoeia in the excerpt. Discuss with students how Poe, in addition to using onomatopoeia, chose his words carefully and repeated them to make them sound like bells ringing. You may want to obtain a copy of the entire poem and read it aloud with the students. Students may also enjoy a choral reading of the poem.

Onomatopoeia

OBJECTIVES

- To introduce onomatopoeia in a literary context
- To present examples of onomatopoeia in well-known poems
- To encourage students to use onomatopoeia in writing
- To show students how onomatopoeia can add interest and variety to language

ONOMATOPOEIA SAMPLER

Before you give a copy of the Onomatopoeia Sampler (page 24) to the students, ask them to suggest sounds that represent a night wind blowing. Write their suggestions on the board. Then read "The Night Wind" out loud. What double meaning does the "Yoooo" have? Ask students to react to the poem. Students can add their own examples of onomatopoeia on a copy of page 56 after they complete activity page 25.

SUGGESTED ACTIVITIES

1. Let small groups of students work together to list as many onomatopoeic words as they can. After each group makes a list of words, assemble the entire class and make a classroom chart of onomatopoeic words.

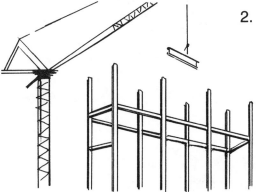

2. Have students write a paragraph using onomatopoeia to describe one of the following scenes:

   space shuttle take-off or landing

   construction of skyscraper

   thunderstorm at night

   morning in the park

   basketball or football game

3. Give pairs of students one of the following sets of words:

clickety clack	*rumble*	*buzz*	*murmuring*	*sizzle*
track	*boom*	*mumble*	*stream*	*drizzle*
choo choo	*crumble*	*bumble*	*dream*	*flapjack*

   Each pair should write a poem using the three words in the set. The poem can be serious or silly, rhyming or free verse. Let students read the poems to their classmates.

ACTIVITY PAGE 25

Students first write a poem using onomatopoeia. Then they design a "new" animal and write a story or poem about it.

Onomatopoeia Sampler

The Night Wind

Have you ever heard the wind go "Yooooo"?
  'Tis a pitiful sound to hear!
It seems to chill you through and through
  With a strange and speechless fear.
'Tis the voice of the night that broods outside
  When folk should be asleep,
And many and many's the time I've cried
To the darkness brooding far and wide
  Over the land the deep:
  "Whom do you want, O lonely night,
  That you wail the long hour through?"
And the night would say in its ghostly way:
    "Yoooooooo!
    Yoooooooo!
    Yoooooooo!"

My mother told me long ago
   (When I was a little tad)
That when the night went wailing so,
   Somebody had been bad;
And then, when I was snug in bed,
   Whither I had been sent,
With the blankets pulled up round my head,
I'd think of what my mother'd said,
   And wonder what boy she meant!
And "Who's been bad to-day?" I'd ask
   Of the wind that hoarsely blew,
And the voice would say in its meaningful way:
    "Yoooooooo!
    Yoooooooo!
    Yoooooooo!"

That this was true I must allow—
   You'll not believe it, though!
Yes, though I'm quite a model now,
   I was not always so.
And if you doubt what thing I say,
   Suppose you make the test;
Suppose, when you've been bad some day
And up to bed are sent away
   From mother and the rest—
Suppose you ask, "Who has been bad?"
   And then you'll hear what's true;
For the wind will moan in its ruefulest tone:
    "Yoooooooo!
    Yoooooooo!
    Yoooooooo!"

—*Eugene Field*

NAME _____

Fun Words

Onomatopoeia makes our language fun to hear and say. For example, say the word "buzz" aloud. What does this word make you think about? Perhaps you can picture this scene:

A big bumblebee buzzes and buzzes around your head. You scream and try to get out of its path, but the bee dives in and stings your arm. You slap and swat the buzzing, mumbling, rumbling bumblebee. Soon the welt on your arm starts to sting and burn, and you begin to moan and groan and wail.

How many onomatopoeic words did you notice in the scene above? Write them on the line below.

_____

Use some or all of the ideas from the scene above to write a short poem about the bee. Use onomatopoeic words in your poem. You can make the poem rhyme or use free verse. Write your first draft on the back of this paper. Work with a partner to revise and edit your poem. When you have finished, share your poem with your classmates.

Onomatopoeia Animal

Have you ever wanted to design a new animal? On a piece of scrap paper, jot down several notes as you read the questions below.

1. What is the size, color, and shape of your animal?

2. How is it like other animals?

3. How is it different from other animals?

4. Does it have any eyes, ears, legs, wings, feet, claws, or paws? If so, how many? What do they look like?

5. What unusual features does your animal have?

6. How does your animal act or behave? What does it do?

7. What onomatopoeic words describe the sounds your animal makes when it's happy? when it's sad? (You can make up new onomatopoeic words if you like.)

8. What onomatopoeic words describe the way your animal walks or moves?

9. What onomatopoeic words describe the way other animals or people respond to your animal?

Use a piece of paper to write a poem or a story about your creation. Include several onomatopoeic words in your writing. When you are satisfied with your poem or story, write the final version on a copy of page 56. You may want to draw a picture of your animal next to your poem or story.

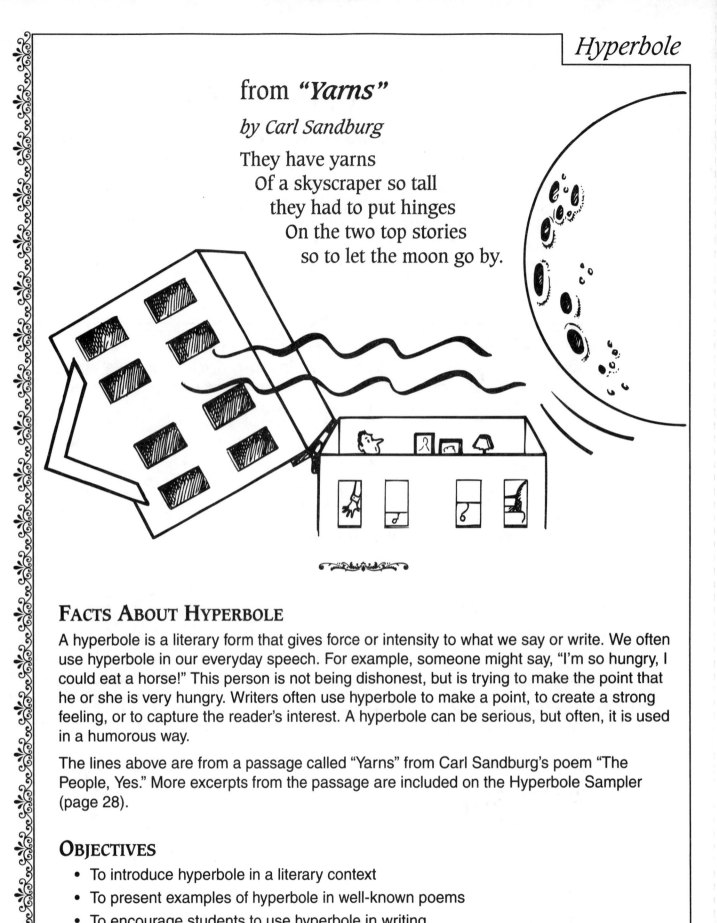

from *"Yarns"*

by Carl Sandburg

They have yarns
   Of a skyscraper so tall
    they had to put hinges
   On the two top stories
    so to let the moon go by.

FACTS ABOUT HYPERBOLE

A hyperbole is a literary form that gives force or intensity to what we say or write. We often use hyperbole in our everyday speech. For example, someone might say, "I'm so hungry, I could eat a horse!" This person is not being dishonest, but is trying to make the point that he or she is very hungry. Writers often use hyperbole to make a point, to create a strong feeling, or to capture the reader's interest. A hyperbole can be serious, but often, it is used in a humorous way.

The lines above are from a passage called "Yarns" from Carl Sandburg's poem "The People, Yes." More excerpts from the passage are included on the Hyperbole Sampler (page 28).

OBJECTIVES

- To introduce hyperbole in a literary context
- To present examples of hyperbole in well-known poems
- To encourage students to use hyperbole in writing
- To show students how hyperbole can add interest and variety to language

Hyperbole

HYPERBOLE SAMPLER

Give each student a copy of the Hyperbole Sampler on page 28. The first poem, "Yarns," includes more excerpts from Carl Sandburg's poem. Discuss the term "yarns." Then read the poem with the students. Students may know more yarns that could be added to the poem. Some students may enjoy illustrating a part of the poem.

"The Ostrich Is a Silly Bird" is a short, silly poem. Encourage students to write a similar poem about another animal. They can write it on a copy of page 56.

SUGGESTED ACTIVITIES

1. Many common expressions use hyperbole. Tell students that although these expressions are exaggerated, there is an element of truth to each one. For example, the hyperbole, "I'm dying of thirst," means that the person is very thirsty. Let students brainstorm a list of such expressions, then discuss and "translate" each of the following expressions:

   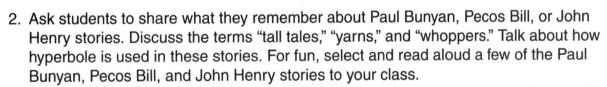

   There were a million people ahead of me in line.
   I've been waiting for hours and hours.
   She's older than the hills.
   It's raining cats and dogs.
   I tossed and turned all night.
   I almost died from embarrassment.
   You could have knocked me over with a feather.

2. Ask students to share what they remember about Paul Bunyan, Pecos Bill, or John Henry stories. Discuss the terms "tall tales," "yarns," and "whoppers." Talk about how hyperbole is used in these stories. For fun, select and read aloud a few of the Paul Bunyan, Pecos Bill, and John Henry stories to your class.

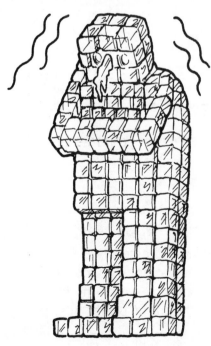

3. As a class, write a group poem entitled "Our Classroom." Write the title and the words below on an overhead transparency. Work together to create a poem that includes both hyperbole and description.

   At times, our classroom seems . . .

as big as . . .	*as small as . . .*
louder than . . .	*quieter than . . .*
colder than . . .	*hotter than . . .*
as sad as . . .	*as happy as . . .*

ACTIVITY PAGE 29

Students first write a "fish story," then they use hyperbole to complete sentences.

Hyperbole Sampler

They have yarns
    Of a skyscraper so tall
        they had to put hinges
           On the two top stories
                so to let the moon go by,
Of one corn crop in Missouri when the roots
    Went so deep and drew off so much water
        The Mississippi riverbed that year was dry,
Of pancakes so thin
    they had only one side,
Of the man who drove a swarm of bees
    across the Rocky Mountains and the Desert
        "and didn't lose a bee."
Of the boy who climbed a cornstalk
    growing so fast he would have starved to death
        if they hadn't shot biscuits up to him,
Of the ship captain's shadow:
    it froze to the deck
        one cold winter night,
Of the sheep-counter
    who was fast and accurate:
        "I just count their feet and divide by four,"
Of mosquitoes:
    one can kill a dog,
        two of them a man,
Of the man who killed a snake
    by putting its tail in its mouth
        so it swallowed itself,
Of Paul Bunyan's big blue ox, Babe,
    measuring between the eyes
        forty-two ax-handles and a plug
           of Star tobacco exactly,
Of John Henry's hammer
    and the curve of its swing
        and his singing of it
           as "a rainbow round my shoulder." They have yarns . . .

excerpts from "Yarns," from "The People, Yes" —*Carl Sandburg*

The Ostrich Is a Silly Bird—*Mary E. Wilkins Freeman*

The ostrich is a silly bird,
    With scarcely any mind.
He often runs so very fast,
    He leaves himself behind.

And when he gets there, has to stand
    And hang about till night,
Without a blessed thing to do
    Until he comes in sight.

Sounds "Fishy" to Me

Did you ever hear of a fish story where the fish is just "a little bigger" than it was when it was caught? Read the fish story below that Mort tells Marta.

Mort: You wouldn't believe the fish I caught the other day. Why, as sure as I stand here, that fish must have been at least 3 feet long and weighed around 24 pounds or so. Let me tell you, that fish fed my whole family for at least a week. It could have fed us for another week, but you know, it was starting to smell a little.

Marta can tell a pretty good fish story herself. On the lines below, write the fish story that Marta tells Mort. Use the back of the paper if you need more space.

_____

_____

_____

_____

_____

Sometimes writers exaggerate (use hyperbole) to make a point. Use hyperbole to complete each sentence below.

The runners on our track team are faster than . . .

_____

My dog is the smartest dog in the whole world. He's so smart that . . .

_____

The loud noise was scarier than . . .

_____

The swimming pool was very little. It was so small that . . .

_____

The new shopping mall was huge. In fact, it was so big that . . .

_____

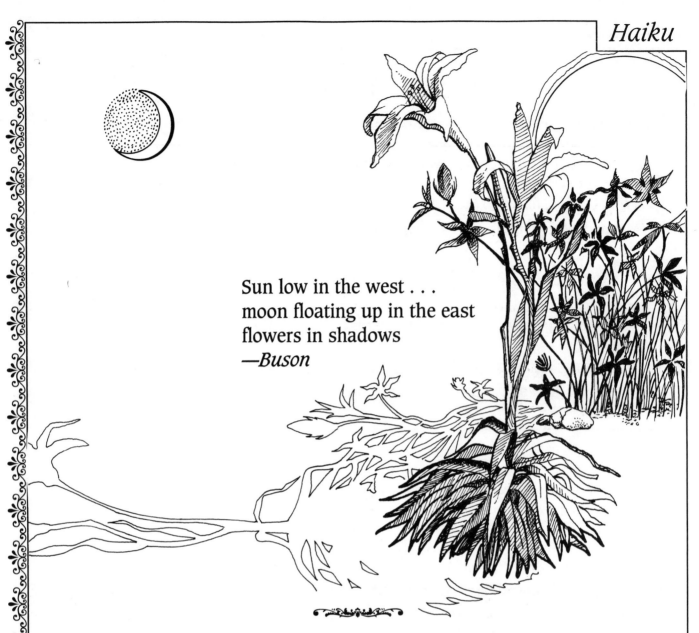

Sun low in the west . . .
moon floating up in the east
flowers in shadows
—*Buson*

FACTS ABOUT HAIKU

Haiku is an ancient poetry style that originated in Japan. For entertainment, courtiers would make up long poems with many parts or stanzas. The first stanzas of the poems were called *hokkus* and described the season and place in which the poem was composed. Eventually, some *hokkus* were published separately.

French diplomats in Japan liked the poems and took them back to France. They became quite popular there, and by the end of the nineteenth century, the *hokkus* were called haiku. From France, the poem form spread to England and America.

A haiku is short, but it does two things:

1. it usually describes a natural object;
2. it includes a second image or an insight that gives energy to the first image.

Traditionally, there are 17 syllables in a haiku. The first line has five syllables, the second line has seven syllables, and the third line has five syllables. Not all haiku poems follow this format, as you can see on the Haiku Sampler (page 32).

Haiku

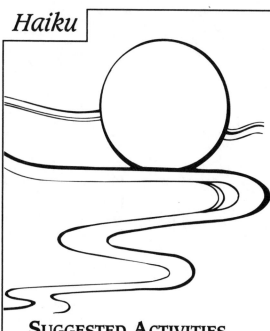

OBJECTIVES

- To identify important characteristics of haiku
- To create original haiku
- To publish poems in classroom displays

ENJOYING THE POEM

Read the haiku by Buson on page 30 to the students. Ask students what natural object is described (flowers). Have them comment on the illustration. Then discuss the image or insight the writer gives about the natural object. (The flowers are in shadows between the sun going down and the moon rising.)

SUGGESTED ACTIVITIES

1. Before students write their own haiku, distribute copies of the Haiku Sampler (page 32). Read the poems with the students. Ask for reactions to the poems. What do they like and dislike? What images and insights do the poems give? Have students count the syllables in each poem. Students may want to illustrate one of the poems.

2. Have students brainstorm about natural objects. Then model a pre-writing clustering technique by choosing one object and writing it in a circle on the board. Ask students what the object reminds them of; what the object makes them think about; what smells, sounds, or tastes come to mind; or what feelings the object gives them. As students brainstorm about the object, write their words and ideas in other circles and draw lines between related ideas. Tell students that clustering can help them discover images and insights they can use to write haiku.

3. Help students write poems or write your own haiku to share with students. Encourage students to read and revise their poems. Let students write traditional and nontraditional poems. Students can work in pairs to check spelling and punctuation. The Japanese poets did not include punctuation, but it may be added if necessary for clarity.

4. Have students neatly write their favorite haikus on clean sheets of paper. Publish students' poems by displaying them on a wall or bulletin board. Encourage students to read each other's poems. When the displays are taken down, students can share and display them at home. (Students can also write their poems on copies of page 56.)

ACTIVITY PAGE 33

Go over the activity and answer any questions students may have. Tell students to have fun as they experiment with haiku poetry.

Haiku Sampler

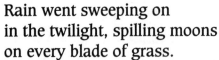

Above the meadow
A skylark, singing, flies high
High into silence.

—*author unknown*

Rain went sweeping on
in the twilight, spilling moons
on every blade of grass.

—*Sho-u*

The sea in springtime—
All the warm day in breathing swells
In breathing swells.

—*Buson*

The spring day closes
Lingering
Where there is water

—*Issa*

Red pepper pods
Add wings to them
And they are dragonflies

—*Basho*

Experimenting With Haiku

List several natural objects you could write about. One object is filled in for you.

1. _clouds_ _____

2. _____

3. _____

4. _____

5. _____

6. _____

Choose one of your objects. Use the back of this page to cluster ideas about your object. First write your object in a circle. Ask yourself these questions:

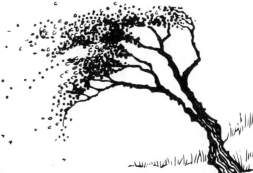

- What does the object remind me of?

- What images or ideas does it make me think of?

- What smells, sounds, and tastes do I think of?

- What feelings does it give me?

Add new ideas in other circles and connect the lines between the circles. Clustering helps you discover images and insights you can use in your poem.

Use the lines below to experiment with haikus. Describe a natural object, and write another idea that gives energy to your first idea. Ask a friend or a writing partner to help you. Try to write one poem using the 17-syllable pattern: five syllables in line one; seven syllables in line two; and five syllables in line three.

_____

_____

_____

_____

Use another sheet of paper to experiment with more haikus. Write your favorite haiku on a copy of page 56 for others to read.

Captain Kidd

by Rosemary and Stephen Vincent Benet

This person in the gaudy clothes
    Is worthy Captain Kidd.
        They say he never buried gold.
          I think, perhaps, he did.

They say it's all a story that
    His favorite little song,
        Was "Make these lubbers walk the plank!"
          I think, perhaps, they're wrong.

They say he never pirated
    Beneath the Skull-and-Bones.
        He merely traveled for his health
          And spoke in soothing tones.
            In fact, you'll read in nearly all
              The newer history books
                That he was mild as cottage cheese
                  —But I don't like his looks!

Narrative Poems

FACTS ABOUT NARRATIVE POEMS

All narrative poems tell stories. These stories can be about real or fictional events or ordinary or famous people. Kings, queens, knights, explorers, adventurers, soldiers, travelers, and presidents have all been written about in narrative poems. Narrative poems can rhyme or be in free verse.

OBJECTIVES

- To identify important characteristics of narrative poetry
- To create original narrative poetry
- To publish poems in classroom displays

ENJOYING THE POEM

Read the narrative poem "Captain Kidd" by Rosemary and Stephen Vincent Benet on page 34 to the students. Ask students to react to the poem. Who was Captain Kidd? What is the main idea in the poem? Ask students to comment on the illustration.

Rosemary and Stephen Vincent Benet wrote many narrative poems. Students might enjoy reading some of these poems in the Benets' book, *A Book of Americans.*

SUGGESTED ACTIVITIES

1. Before students write narrative poems of their own, give students copies of the Narrative Poem Sampler on page 37. Read the poem, "Nancy Hanks," out loud. As the students read and listen to the poem, ask them to imagine Abe as his mother describes him. Ask students to react to the poem. Do they know who Nancy Hanks is after hearing the poem? Some students might want to illustrate Lincoln as a boy in the space on the handout.

2. Other narrative poems students might enjoy include "Casey at the Bat" by Ernest Lawrence Thayer, "The Listeners" by Walter de la Mare, and "The Ballad of Red Fox" by Melvin Walker La Follette.

3. As a class, brainstorm and list topics that might make good narrative poems. List famous people, historical events, explorers, travelers, kings, queens, magical creatures, etc. Also have students consider local events, people, and history.

4. Have students neatly write their favorite narrative poems on clean sheets of paper. Publish students' poems by displaying them on a wall or bulletin board. Encourage students to read each other's writing. When the papers are taken down, students can share and display them at home. (Students can also write their poems on copies of page 56.)

5. Encourage students to read and share other narrative poems. Obtain a copy of *A Book of Americans* by Rosemary and Stephen Vincent Benet for students to enjoy.

ACTIVITY PAGE 38

Go through the activity with students and tell them that everyone has a story to tell! Their poems can be about real or imaginary persons or events. Circulate around the room to help students with their ideas. Some students may need to complete research about a topic before they begin to write. Let students work cooperatively to read and react to each other's poems. Have them revise poems before copying them onto clean sheets of paper. Encourage students to work in pairs to check spelling and punctuation.

Narrative Poem Sampler

Nancy Hanks

If Nancy Hanks
Came back as a ghost,
Seeking news
Of what she loved most,
She'd ask first
"Where's my son?
What's happened to Abe?
What's he done?

"Poor little Abe, left all alone
Except for Tom
Who's a rolling stone;
He was only nine
The year I died;
I remember still
How hard he cried.

"Scraping along
In a little shack,
With hardly a shirt
To cover his back,
And a prairie wind
To blow him down
Or pinching times
If he went to town.

"You wouldn't know
About my son?
Did he grow tall?
Did he have fun?
Did he learn to read?
Did he get to town?
Do you know his name?
Did he get on?"

—*Rosemary and
Stephen Vincent Benet*

NAME _____

Write a Narrative Poem

List a few topics you could write a narrative poem about.
One has been filled in for you.

1. <u>sailor at sea</u>

2. _____

3. _____

4. _____

5. _____

6. _____

Choose one of the topics you wrote above. Who will the character(s) be? Write his or her name below.

_____

Now think about the story you want to tell. Before you write your poem, summarize what happens at the beginning of the story on the lines below.

_____

_____

Summarize what happens in the middle of the story.

_____

_____

Summarize what happens at the end of the story.

_____

_____

In the poem "Captain Kidd," the poet includes some of Captain Kidd's direct words in quotation marks. You may want to try this technique in your poem. On the lines below, write the direct words of one of your characters.

_____

_____

Use the back of this paper to experiment with writing narrative poems. You may use rhyming words or free verse. Copy your finished poem on a clean sheet of paper for others to read.

Fog

by Carl Sandburg

The fog comes
    on little cat feet.

It sits looking
    over harbor and city
      on silent haunches
        and then moves on.

FACTS ABOUT FREE VERSE

Free verse is easy and fun to write. There isn't any strict verse pattern, nor does free verse poetry rhyme. Instead, free verse lets the writer use language that appeals to the head and the heart. The poet can express his or her feelings, emotions, and ideas in an imaginative way. Free verse poems can be about serious or humorous subjects.

OBJECTIVES

- To identify important characteristics of free verse
- To create original free verse
- To publish poems in classroom displays

ENJOYING THE POEM

Read the free verse poem by Carl Sandburg on page 39. Ask students to react to the poem. What do they like best about it? Do they recognize it as poetry since it doesn't rhyme? What do they think the poem means? Why does the author say the fog comes on little cat feet? Then ask them to comment on the illustration.

SUGGESTED ACTIVITIES

1. Before students write their own free verse poems, give students copies of the Free Verse Sampler on page 41. It features poems by Carl Sandburg and Langston Hughes. Ask students which poem they like best. Why? Which poem would be fun to illustrate? What images (pictures) do the poems evoke? What emotions do the poets express? Students may want to illustrate one or both of the poems.

2. Next, give students a few of the opening lines below and ask them to write a short free verse poem. Ask volunteers to read their poems to the class. Then have students list other topics and first lines they can use to write more free verse poems.

    Getting up on Monday morning . . .

    I spilled a can of orange soda pop.

    The cars on the freeway hum by.

    The summer sun . . .

Publish students' poems by displaying them on a wall or bulletin board.

ACTIVITY PAGE 42

Tell students to have fun as they play with words and ideas while completing this page.

Free Verse Sampler

Buffalo Dusk

The buffaloes are gone.
And those who saw the buffaloes are gone.
Those who saw the buffaloes by the thousands
    and how they pawed the prairie sod into dust
    with their hooves, their great heads down
    pawing on in a great pageant of dusk,
Those who saw the buffaloes are gone.
And the buffaloes are gone.

— *Carl Sandburg*

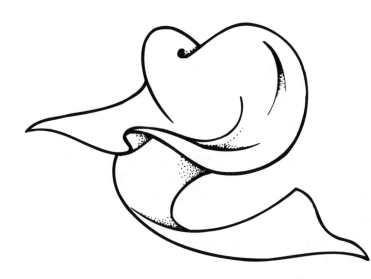

The Dream Keeper

Bring me all of your dreams,
You dreamers,
Bring me all of your
Heart melodies
That I may wrap them
In a blue cloud-cloth
Away from the too-rough fingers
Of the world.

—*Langston Hughes*

Fun With Free Verse

List a few objects you could write about. One has been filled in for you. You may want to write about a childhood memory.

1. _pony in a meadow_
2. _____
3. _____
4. _____
5. _____
6. _____

Select one of your objects. Close your eyes and picture the object. Think about where the object is located. Think about the sights, sounds, colors, tastes, and smells associated with it. On the lines below, write as many descriptive phrases as you can about your object.

location: _____

sights: _____

sounds: _____

colors: _____

tastes: _____

smells: _____

Circle the phrases above that you like best. Cross out or change phrases you dislike.

What emotion do you want to express in your poem?

_____

Write more details (words and phrases) that will give your reader a clear image or picture of the object.

_____

Use the back of this page to arrange the words and phrases into a free verse poem. Ask a friend or writing partner to read your poem and suggest changes that will make your image clearer. Revise your poem by adding or deleting phrases until the poem sounds right to you.

Write your free verse poem on a clean sheet of paper for others to read and enjoy. Then write it on a copy of page 56.

Old Man with a Beard
by Edward Lear

There was an Old Man with a beard
Who said, "It is just as I feared!
Two Owls and a Hen
Four Larks and a Wren,
Have all built their nests in my beard!"

FACTS ABOUT LIMERICKS

A limerick is a five-line poem. The first, second, and fifth lines rhyme and have three beats to the rhythm. The third and fourth lines rhyme and have two beats to the rhythm. Limericks are often silly and humorous. They're great fun to read and even more fun to write!

OBJECTIVES

- To identify important characteristics of limericks
- To create original limericks
- To publish poems in classroom displays

"The Owl and the Pussy Cat"

ENJOYING THE POEM

Read the limerick by Edward Lear on page 43. Ask students to react to the poem. What do they like best about it? Then ask them to comment on the illustration. Let students read the poem out loud several times to hear the rhythm of the lines.

Edward Lear (1812–1888) lived in England. He liked to draw and paint, and he was even Queen Victoria's drawing teacher. In 1846, he wrote and illustrated a fun book of poems called *A Book of Nonsense.*

SUGGESTED ACTIVITIES

1. Before students write their own limericks, give them the Limerick Sampler on page 45. Read the limericks out loud and have students clap or tap out the beats. You may want to write these limericks on a transparency and use the overhead projector. Which limericks do students like best? Why? Are the poems humorous or serious? Which limerick would be fun to illustrate?

2. Give students some of the opening lines below. As a class, complete a few limericks together, so students begin to hear the pattern and rhythm of limericks. Then have students work together in pairs to complete other limericks.

   There was a Young Lady named Lynn . . .
   Some trees grow sideways I'm told . . .
   There once was a mountain too high . . .

3. Circulate around the room to listen to and enjoy students' poems. Write a few limericks of your own to share with your students. Let students work cooperatively to read and react to each other's poems. Have them revise poems before copying them onto clean sheets of paper for display on a wall or bulletin board. Students can work in pairs to check spelling and punctuation.

4. Encourage students to read each other's poems. When the papers are returned, students can share and display them at home. Also have students write their limericks on copies of page 56.

5. Encourage students to read and share other humorous poems. Find a copy of *A Book of Nonsense* by Edward Lear for students to enjoy.

ACTIVITY PAGE 46

Go through this activity and answer any questions students may have. Tell students to have fun as they play with words and ideas.

Limerick Sampler

The bottle of perfume that Willie sent
Was highly displeasing to Millicent;
    Her thanks were so cold
    They quarreled, I'm told,
Through that silly scent Willie sent Millicent.

—*author unknown*

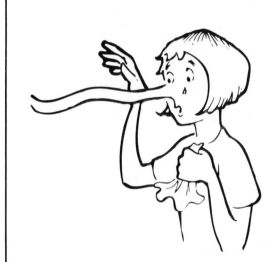

There was a Young Lady whose Nose
Continually prospers and grows;
    When it grew out of sight,
    She exclaimed in a fright,
"Oh! Farewell to the end of my Nose!"

—*Edward Lear*

There was a Young Lady of Niger
Who smiled as she rode on a tiger;
    They returned from the ride
    With the lady inside,
And the smile on the face of the tiger.

—*Edward Lear*

Laughable Limericks

List a few topics you could write about. One has been filled in for you.

1. *a famous person*
2. _____
3. _____
4. _____
5. _____
6. _____

"A horse with a very long tail"

Choose one of your topics. Write the first line of your limerick below. Try to tap out the beats softly with your pencil. (There should be three beats.)

_____

Think of words that rhyme with the last word in your first line. This will help you write the next line. On the back of this paper, write words that rhyme with the last word in your first line.

Now write the second line of your poem. Check for three beats.

_____

Write the third and fourth lines. These two lines are shorter and end with a different rhyme than the first two lines. Each line has two beats. Use the back of this paper to write rhyming words again.

_____

_____

Now write the last line of your poem. It should rhyme with the first two lines. It has three beats.

_____

Try writing another limerick on the back of this paper. Write your best limerick on a clean sheet of paper for others to read. Then write it on a copy of page 56.

Who Has Seen the Wind?
by Christina Rossetti

Who has seen the wind?
  Neither I nor you:
    But when the leaves hang trembling,
      The wind is passing through.

Who has seen the wind?
  Neither you nor I:
    But when the trees blow down their heads,
      The wind is passing by.

FACTS ABOUT LYRIC POEMS

Lyric poetry developed from an ancient Greek form of poetry that was accompanied by a musical instrument, usually a lyre. These types of poems are like songs and have a musical quality about them.

Lyric poems appeal to our senses and emotions. They are personal, subjective poems. By choosing words and phrases carefully, you can set the mood for a lyric poem. Lyric poems can rhyme or be in free verse.

OBJECTIVES

- To identify important characteristics of lyric poetry
- To create original lyric poetry
- To publish poems in classroom displays

ENJOYING THE POEM

Read to the students the lyric poem "Who Has Seen the Wind?" by Christina Rossetti on page 47. Ask students to react to the poem. Do they like or dislike it? Then ask them to comment on the illustration.

SUGGESTED ACTIVITIES

1. Before students write lyric poems, give them copies of the Lyric Poem Sampler on page 49. Read the poems out loud. As the students listen to and read the poems, ask them to think about what senses or emotions the poet is writing about. Have the students use these thoughts to illustrate each of the poems.

   Which poem do students like best? Discuss the musical quality of each poem. Students might better understand the idea of lyric poetry by comparing it with the lyrics (words) in songs.

2. As a class, brainstorm and list topics that might make good lyric poems. Consider topics in categories such as seasons of the year, virtues, qualities, nature, animals, musical sounds, etc.

3. Circulate around the room to listen to and enjoy students' poems. Write a few lyric poems of your own to share with students. Let students work cooperatively to read and react to each other's poems. Let them revise poems before they copy them onto clean sheets of paper for display on a wall or bulletin board.

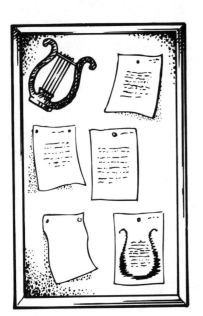

4. Encourage students to read each other's poems. When the papers are returned, students can share and display them at home. Also have students write their own lyric poems on copies of page 56.

5. Encourage students to read and share other lyrical poems.

ACTIVITY PAGE 50

Go through this activity with students and tell them that they will be writing lyric poems that start with a question and use a pattern similar to that used in "Who Has Seen the Wind?" Ask students to think in a lighthearted, musical way.

Lyric Poem Sampler

April

The roofs are shining from the rain,
    The sparrows twitter as they fly,
And with a windy April grace
    The little clouds go by.

Yet the backyards are bare and brown
    With only one unchanging tree—
I could not be so sure of Spring
    Save that it sings in me.

—*Sara Teasdale*

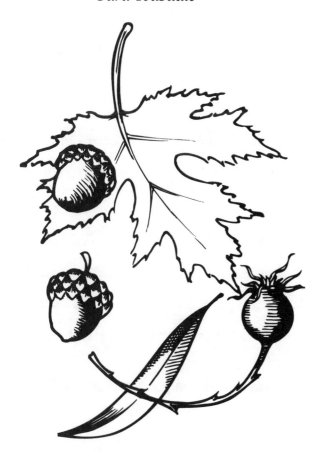

Autumn

The morns are meeker than they were,
    The nuts are getting brown;
The berry's cheek is plumper,
    The rose is out of town.

The maple wears a gayer scarf,
    The field a scarlet gown,
Lest I should be old-fashioned,
    I'll put a trinket on.

—*Emily Dickinson*

NAME _____

Write a Lyric Poem

List a few topics you could write about.
One has been filled in for you.

1.   _summer_ _____

2.   _____

3.   _____

4.   _____

5.   _____

6.   _____

Circle the topic you like best. Now write a few words or phrases about your topic. For example, if "summer" is your topic, you could write "hot sun, picnics, and swimming."

Your words:

_____

What emotion or feeling do you want your poem to have?

_____

One easy way to start is to write a question about your topic. This will be the first line of your poem. Here is an example: "Is summer really here?"

Your question:

_____

Write three more lines, answering your question. You may want to make the first and third lines rhyme and the second and fourth lines rhyme. Use the back of this paper to experiment before you write your lines below.

_____

_____

_____

Try to write a second verse (stanza) to your poem. You can start the stanza by writing another question or just use the same question again.

Now try writing another lyric poem on the back of this paper. When you are done, write it on a copy of page 56.

Baseball
by Cindy Barden

Baseball
Bat cracks against
The pitch, sending it out
Over the back fence, I did it!
Homerun

FACTS ABOUT CINQUAINS

In some ways, cinquains are similar to haiku. Both cinquains and haiku are short poems that follow a set pattern. Like haiku, cinquains are often about nature, but many authors write about other topics, too. Cinquain poems do not rhyme.

The inventor of the cinquain was Adalaide Crapsey (1878–1914). Cinquains have five lines. The number of syllables in successive lines are two, four, six, eight, and two. This pattern is used in the poem on page 51. "November Night" by Adalaide Crapsey (page 54) also uses this pattern. Below are two other popular patterns for writing cinquains.

Dinosaurs
by Cindy Barden

Line 1: One word	Dinosaurs
Line 2: Two words	Lived once,
Line 3: Three words	Long ago, but
Line 4: Four words	Only dust and dreams
Line 5: One word	Remain

Spaghetti
by Cindy Barden

Line 1: A noun	Spaghetti
Line 2: Two adjectives	Messy, spicy
Line 3: Three words ending in -ing	Slurping, sliding, falling
Line 4: A phrase	Between my plate and mouth
Line 5: Another word for the noun	Delicious

It can be fun for students to experiment with all three patterns.

OBJECTIVES

- To identify important characteristics of cinquains
- To create original cinquains
- To publish poems in classroom displays

ENJOYING THE POEM

Read the cinquain "Baseball" by Cindy Barden on page 51. What do students like about this poem? What action takes place in the poem? What feeling does the poem give? Ask students to comment on the illustration.

SUGGESTED ACTIVITIES

1. Before students write their own cinquains, give them copies of the Cinquain Sampler on page 54. Ask for student reactions. Which cinquain do students like best? Why? Which pattern do they think will be easiest to write? Students may want to illustrate one of the poems.

2. Brainstorm with students about possible topics for their own cinquains. Write their suggestions on the overhead or board.

3. Circulate around the room to listen to and enjoy students' poems. Write a few cinquains of your own to share with your students. Let students work cooperatively to read and react to each other's poems. Have them revise poems before copying them onto clean sheets of paper for display on a wall or bulletin board.

4. Encourage students to read each other's poems. When the papers are returned, students can share and display them at home. Also have students write their poems on copies of page 56.

ACTIVITY PAGE 55

Go through this activity and answer any questions. Tell students to experiment with all three patterns.

Cinquain Sampler

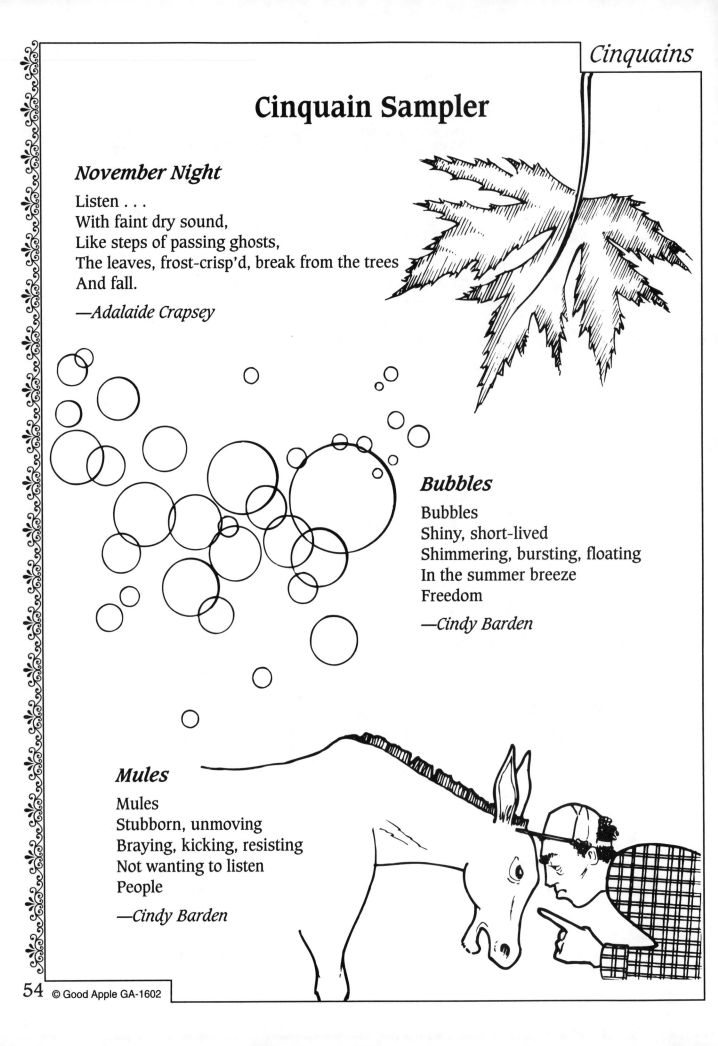

November Night

Listen . . .
With faint dry sound,
Like steps of passing ghosts,
The leaves, frost-crisp'd, break from the trees
And fall.

—*Adalaide Crapsey*

Bubbles

Bubbles
Shiny, short-lived
Shimmering, bursting, floating
In the summer breeze
Freedom

—*Cindy Barden*

Mules

Mules
Stubborn, unmoving
Braying, kicking, resisting
Not wanting to listen
People

—*Cindy Barden*

NAME _____

Cinquain Patterns

On the back of this paper, list three topics you could write about. Write as many words and phrases as you can think of for each topic. Pick one of your topics. Write a cinquain using Pattern #1, Pattern #2, or Pattern #3.

Pattern #1

Line 1: Two syllables
Line 2: Four syllables
Line 3: Six syllables
Line 4: Eight syllables
Line 5: Two syllables

Pattern #2

Line 1: One word
Line 2: Two words
Line 3: Three words
Line 4: Four words
Line 5: One word

Pattern #3

Line 1: Noun
Line 2: Two adjectives
Line 3: Three words ending in *-ing*
Line 4: A phrase
Line 5: Another word for the noun

_____

_____

_____

_____

_____

Use the same topic or another topic. Write a cinquain in a different pattern than you used above.

_____

_____

_____

_____

_____

Write your favorite cinquain below for others to read and enjoy.

_____

_____

_____

_____

Writing Paper POETRY ✳ HAIKU ✳ CINQUAIN ❖ LIMERICK

✳ NARRATIVE ❖ POETRY ✎ FREE VERSE ❖ CINQUAIN ✎ ONOMATOPOEIA ✳

ONOMATOPOEIA ❖ HYPERBOLE ❖ ALLITERATION ✎ METAPHOR ❖ IRONY

PERSONIFICATION ❖ LYRIC ✎ FREE VERSE

56